90-DAY GOALS JOURNAL

90-DAY GOALS JOURNAL

A Daily Check-In to Stay Motivated and on Track

Emily Cassel

ROCKRIDGE PRESS

This book belongs to:

____

For general information on our other products and services or to obtain technical support, please contact our Customer Care Department within the United States at (866) 744-2665, or outside the United States at (510) 253-0500.

Rockridge Press publishes its books in a variety of electronic and print formats. Some content that appears in print may not be available in electronic books, and vice versa.

Cover and Interior Designer: Lori Cervone
Art Producer: Melissa Malinowks
Editor: Olivia Bartz
Production Editor: Ellina Litmanovich
Production Manager: Riley Hoffman

All Illustrations used under license © Curly_Pat/Creative Market. Author Photo Courtesy of Madison Krupp Photography

Paperback ISBN: 978-1-63807-357-4
R0

Contents

Introduction

Welcome to the 90-Day Goals Journal! I'm so excited and grateful to be your guide. I'm Emily Cassel, Soulful Business + Leadership Coach for women entrepreneurs. My background is in positive psychology, sustainability, entrepreneurship, and spirituality, and I've been working with clients since 2014 to create world-changing impact and set themselves free from everything that holds them back. In both my personal and professional lives I have observed the critical importance of setting goals and having a system of accountability around pursuing and, ultimately, achieving them. The benefits of setting goals include greater focus, motivation, direction, and clarity around what matters most to you. But, finding the motivation to build new habits or break old ones can be really hard. This journal will walk you through how to set, track, and meet your goals over a manageable 90-day period with prompts to keep your goals at the forefront of your mind and plenty of positive encouragement along the way to keep you moving forward. The process of setting goals, tracking your progress, and seeing how far you've come is a deeply fulfilling one, and I'm so happy that this journal can act as a resource and companion for you over the next 90 days!

How to Use This Journal

Setting and pursuing goals can be an experience of great courage, fulfillment, and growth when you feel equipped with the right tools and structure to set, pursue, and achieve your goals. In the forthcoming sections, I'll walk you through how to set powerful goals thoroughly and with intention, so that they are S.M.A.R.T.: Specific, Measurable, Attainable, Relevant, and Time-oriented. Once you've identified the goals that matter most to you and set them using this proven S.M.A.R.T. system, the tracker pages that follow will support you to put your goals into action.

At the start of each week, you'll be prompted to set a micro-goal that relates to your overarching goal(s) for the duration of this journal. Each day in the tracker is divided evenly into a set of prompts designed to be filled in at the start of your day and a set to be filled in at the end of your day. Each morning, you'll be asked to identify three action steps that will support you in achieving your weekly micro-goal in the morning, and you'll be invited to reflect on your progress and growth in the evening. At the end of each week, you'll reflect on your progress, make any necessary adjustments to stay on course, and realign with your intentions and goals where needed. I've also included an inspiring weekly affirmation that you can use to stay focused and motivated as a mantra, or repetitive phrase you can come back to as a touchstone or reminder of what matters, throughout the week. First, we'll take a closer look at the S.M.A.R.T. system to help you set an effective, focused, and clear goal.

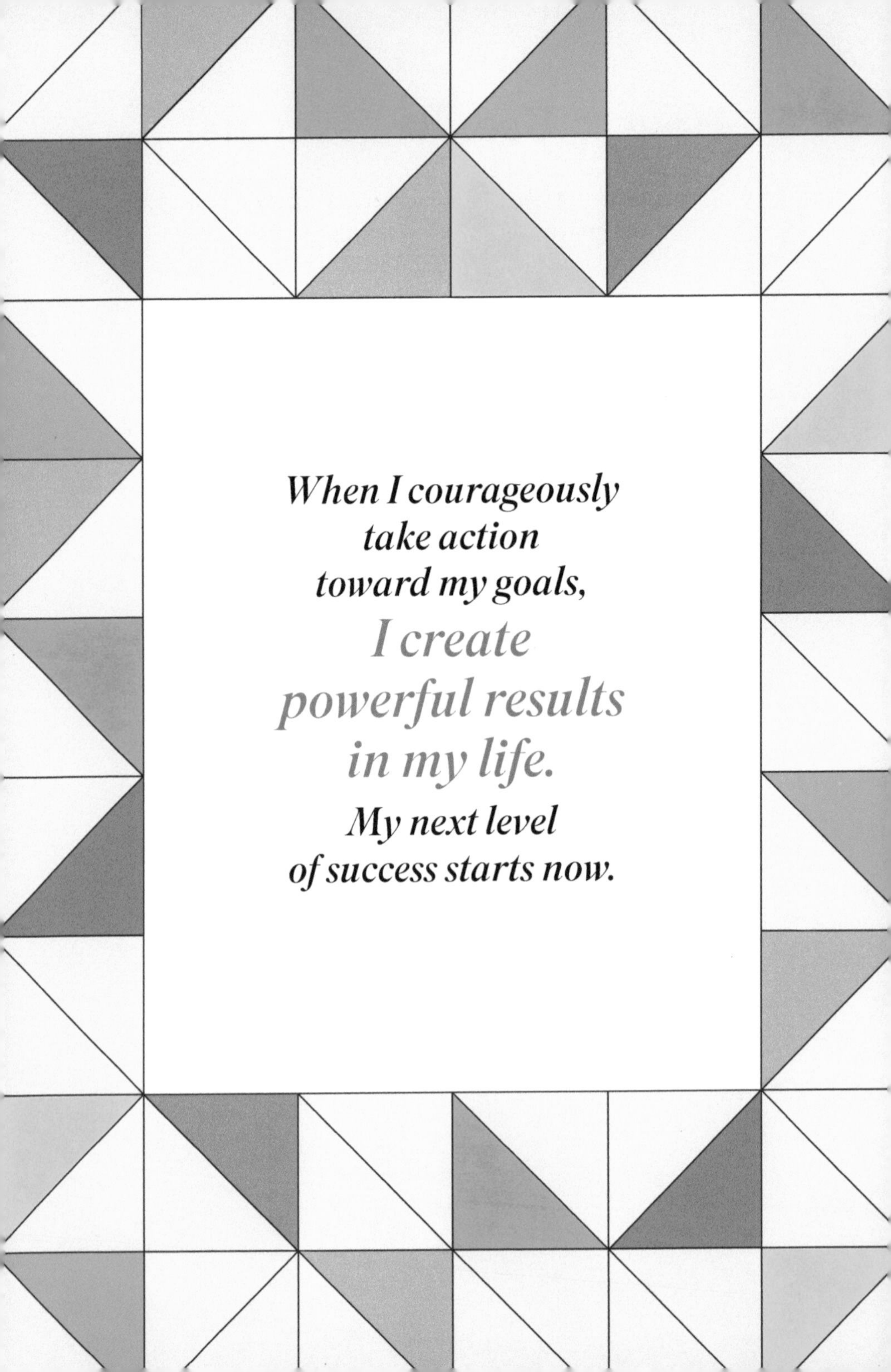
When I courageously
take action
toward my goals,
I create
powerful results
in my life.
My next level
of success starts now.

PART I

Start the S.M.A.R.T. Way

Have you ever felt frustrated by the idea of goal-setting? Perhaps it felt overwhelming, or you felt unclear about how to do it in a way that enabled you to know when and if you'd achieved your goal. If this sounds familiar, you're certainly not alone! Without the correct phrasing of your goals, you can feel like the goals you set become unfulfilled moving targets that you never quite feel a sense of accomplishment or satisfaction around, because you don't know whether you've actually achieved them. In the past, it is likely that you have set goals in a vague way that leaves you feeling less than inspired to take action toward them and as if you've already failed, instead of energized and confident in your abilities to pursue similar (or bigger, more daring) goals in the future. There are five key elements involved in establishing effective goals that set you up for success while allowing you to feel much more clear, focused, and motivated in your pursuit of achieving them. In order for a goal to be optimal, it needs to follow the S.M.A.R.T. system and be Specific, Measurable, Attainable, Relevant, and Time-oriented.

Specify Your Goal

For your goal to be specific and clear, it should answer at least one of the 5 W's: who, what, when, where, and why. Consider this the "mission statement" for your goal. What do you want to accomplish, create, do, or become, and why is it important to you? Instead of "I want to be nicer," aim for something more specific, like "I want to create a more loving and fulfilling relationship with my partner."

Make Your Goal Measurable

For your goal to be measurable, consider what it would actually look like to have achieved it. What is the metric you'll use to measure whether or not you've reached your goal successfully? Providing a way to measure progress makes a goal more tangible. How will you know that you've achieved your goal? What is the metric you'll be measuring to know for certain that you've reached it?

Instead of a general goal like "I want to eat healthier," aim for something more measurable, like "I want to eat two plant-based meals a day and reduce my coffee consumption by 50 percent."

Choose Something Attainable

Making your goal attainable helps prevent frustration or burnout so that your goal can be realistically achievable for you. Some things to consider are whether the amount of skill and effort required to achieve the goal are manageable. For example, do you have the skills already, or will you need to develop and obtain them? If you do not already possess the required skills, knowledge, beliefs, or attitudes to achieve your goal, how will you acquire them? Will the amount of effort you put into this goal create a worthwhile outcome that matters to you? The intention here is to set goals that are inspiring, not discouraging, so be sure to set a goal that's realistic so you can follow through.

Consider your goal thoughtfully and make sure it's something you can realistically achieve (e.g., if you want to replace your phone-scrolling habit with reading, aim for setting an attainable goal, like "Read for 15 minutes before bed" rather than "Read one book a day").

Check Your Goal's Relevance

For your goal to be relevant, it needs to connect to and align with your bigger picture. Does this goal make sense in the context of the rest of your life? Is it connected to a greater intention, purpose, mission, or desire you have? There are plenty of things you could pursue, but few are truly relevant to the bigger picture of your life, objectives, and desires. How does your goal connect to and align with your overarching intention and purpose?

Reflect on what your goal means to you specifically, making sure that the goal is meaningful to you and your lifestyle rather than others' opinions, societal conditioning, or what you think you "should" be pursuing.

Time-Stamp Your Goal

For your goal to be time-bound, it needs to answer the questions "When will this happen? What is the deadline?" Without a sense of urgency, the goal will likely never be achieved because it remains an idea, dream, or wish without a solid plan. When you assign a deadline and time constraint, you can start planning and taking action toward the desired outcome and witness your progress over time. Building on the attainability prompt, think about how long it would take you to realistically reach your goal. Choose a time frame that feels challenging yet energizing.

I am ready, willing, and capable of achieving my goals.

Every moment
is a chance
to choose progress
over resistance.

PART II

Get Goal-ing!

Throughout the pages that follow, I've made it as easy as possible for you to track your progress and stay on course to achieve the S.M.A.R.T. goal(s) you've just identified for the next 90 days! I've taken out all the guesswork, so all you have to do is open this journal once in the morning and once at night each day and follow the prompts. At the end of each week, you'll reflect and identify what's working, what's getting in the way of achieving your goals, and what needs to be adjusted within your approach so you can stay on track. By keeping your S.M.A.R.T. goal(s) top of mind throughout the next 90 days, you'll learn a wealth of knowledge about yourself, your patterns (both helpful and unhelpful), and what inspires you to keep going in the midst of a challenge. Whether you achieve the exact goal you've identified today, or whether that goal shifts and changes as you progress through these pages, you'll be equipped with the skills, tools, and system to change course without skipping a beat. My hope is that the skills you learn, progress you make, and tools you acquire here will serve you for the rest of your life and will translate into everything you do from now on so that you can live your most fulfilling and successful life.

DAY 1 Date ______

Morning

My top priority goal for this week is: ______

The three most critical actions I can take today to achieve this result:

- ❑ ______
- ❑ ______
- ❑ ______

Next Steps

Evening

Something I am grateful for that helped propel me forward today:

Something I learned I can improve moving forward:

Notes & Thoughts

DAY 2 Date

Morning

My top priority goal for this week is:

The three most critical actions I can take today to achieve this result:

- ❑
- ❑
- ❑

Next Steps

Evening

Something I am grateful for that helped propel me forward today:

Something I learned I can improve moving forward:

Notes & Thoughts

DAY 3 Date

Morning

My top priority goal for this week is:

The three most critical actions I can take today to achieve this result:

- ❑
- ❑
- ❑

Next Steps

Evening

Something I am grateful for that helped propel me forward today:

Something I learned I can improve moving forward:

Notes & Thoughts

DAY 4 Date

Morning

My top priority goal for this week is:

The three most critical actions I can take today to achieve this result:

- ❑
- ❑
- ❑

Next Steps

Evening

Something I am grateful for that helped propel me forward today:

Something I learned I can improve moving forward:

Notes & Thoughts

DAY 5 Date

Morning

My top priority goal for this week is:

The three most critical actions I can take today to achieve this result:

- ☐
- ☐
- ☐

Next Steps

Evening

Something I am grateful for that helped propel me forward today:

Something I learned I can improve moving forward:

Notes & Thoughts

DAY 6

Date

Morning

My top priority goal for this week is:

The three most critical actions I can take today to achieve this result:

- ❑
- ❑
- ❑

Next Steps

Evening

Something I am grateful for that helped propel me forward today:

Something I learned I can improve moving forward:

Notes & Thoughts

DAY 7 Check-In

Did you accomplish last week's goal? YES ❑ NO ❑

On a scale of 1 to 10 (1 = least amount of effort, 10 = most amount of effort), how much effort did you commit to achieving last week's goal? ______

What did you learn about yourself in the process of pursuing last week's goal, regardless of the outcome? ______

What is one habit, thought, pattern, behavior, or practice that you've learned works well for you and feels supportive in pursuit of your goal? What's something that feels unsupportive, or as though it counteracts your progress in pursuit of your goal?

How are you committed to shifting your approach to accomplishing next week's goal? ______

What would it look like for you to show up fully (at a level 10 effort) toward next week's goal? List specific actions you'll START or STOP doing next week.

Based on your progress this week, what is one micro-goal you are committed to completing next week?

When you achieve next week's goal, how will you reward yourself and celebrate your progress?

I AM ABUNDANTLY SUPPORTED IN MY PURSUIT OF WHAT MATTERS MOST TO ME.

DAY 8 Date

Morning

My top priority goal for this week is:

The three most critical actions I can take today to achieve this result:

- ❑
- ❑
- ❑

Next Steps

Evening

Something I am grateful for that helped propel me forward today:

Something I learned I can improve moving forward:

Notes & Thoughts

DAY 9 Date

Morning

My top priority goal for this week is:

The three most critical actions I can take today to achieve this result:

- ❑
- ❑
- ❑

Next Steps

Evening

Something I am grateful for that helped propel me forward today:

Something I learned I can improve moving forward:

Notes & Thoughts

DAY 10 Date

Morning

My top priority goal for this week is:

The three most critical actions I can take today to achieve this result:

- [ ]
- [ ]
- [ ]

Next Steps

Evening

Something I am grateful for that helped propel me forward today:

Something I learned I can improve moving forward:

Notes & Thoughts

DAY 11 Date

Morning

My top priority goal for this week is:

The three most critical actions I can take today to achieve this result:

- ❑
- ❑
- ❑

Next Steps

Evening

Something I am grateful for that helped propel me forward today:

Something I learned I can improve moving forward:

Notes & Thoughts

DAY 12 Date

Morning

My top priority goal for this week is:

The three most critical actions I can take today to achieve this result:

- ❑
- ❑
- ❑

Next Steps

Evening

Something I am grateful for that helped propel me forward today:

Something I learned I can improve moving forward:

Notes & Thoughts

DAY 13 Date

Morning

My top priority goal for this week is:

The three most critical actions I can take today to achieve this result:

- ❑
- ❑
- ❑

Next Steps

Evening

Something I am grateful for that helped propel me forward today:

Something I learned I can improve moving forward:

Notes & Thoughts

DAY 14 Check-In

Did you accomplish last week's goal? YES ❑ NO ❑

On a scale of 1 to 10 (1 = least amount of effort, 10 = most amount of effort), how much effort did you commit to achieving last week's goal? ______

What did you learn about yourself in the process of pursuing last week's goal, regardless of the outcome? ______

What is one habit, thought, pattern, behavior, or practice that you've learned works well for you and feels supportive in pursuit of your goal? What's something that feels unsupportive, or as though it counteracts your progress in pursuit of your goal?

How are you committed to shifting your approach to accomplishing next week's goal? ______

What would it look like for you to show up fully (at a level 10 effort) toward next week's goal? List specific actions you'll START or STOP doing next week.

Based on your progress this week, what is one micro-goal you are committed to completing next week?

When you achieve next week's goal, how will you reward yourself and celebrate your progress?

I TRUST MYSELF TO HONOR AND FOLLOW THROUGH ON THE COMMITMENTS I MAKE TO MYSELF.

DAY 15 Date

Morning

My top priority goal for this week is:

The three most critical actions I can take today to achieve this result:

- ❑
- ❑
- ❑

Next Steps

Evening

Something I am grateful for that helped propel me forward today:

Something I learned I can improve moving forward:

Notes & Thoughts

DAY 16 Date

Morning

My top priority goal for this week is:

The three most critical actions I can take today to achieve this result:

- ❑
- ❑
- ❑

Next Steps

Evening

Something I am grateful for that helped propel me forward today:

Something I learned I can improve moving forward:

Notes & Thoughts

DAY 17 Date

Morning

My top priority goal for this week is:

The three most critical actions I can take today to achieve this result:

- [ ]
- [ ]
- [ ]

Next Steps

Evening

Something I am grateful for that helped propel me forward today:

Something I learned I can improve moving forward:

Notes & Thoughts

DAY 18 Date

Morning

My top priority goal for this week is:

The three most critical actions I can take today to achieve this result:

- ❑
- ❑
- ❑

Next Steps

Evening

Something I am grateful for that helped propel me forward today:

Something I learned I can improve moving forward:

Notes & Thoughts

DAY 19 Date

Morning

My top priority goal for this week is:

The three most critical actions I can take today to achieve this result:

- ❑
- ❑
- ❑

Next Steps

Evening

Something I am grateful for that helped propel me forward today:

Something I learned I can improve moving forward:

Notes & Thoughts

DAY 20 Date

Morning

My top priority goal for this week is:

The three most critical actions I can take today to achieve this result:

- ❑
- ❑
- ❑

Next Steps

Evening

Something I am grateful for that helped propel me forward today:

Something I learned I can improve moving forward:

Notes & Thoughts

DAY 21 Check-In

Did you accomplish last week's goal? YES ☐ NO ☐

On a scale of 1 to 10 (1 = least amount of effort, 10 = most amount of effort), how much effort did you commit to achieving last week's goal? ______

What did you learn about yourself in the process of pursuing last week's goal, regardless of the outcome? ______

What is one habit, thought, pattern, behavior, or practice that you've learned works well for you and feels supportive in pursuit of your goal? What's something that feels unsupportive, or as though it counteracts your progress in pursuit of your goal?

How are you committed to shifting your approach to accomplishing next week's goal? ______

What would it look like for you to show up fully (at a level 10 effort) toward next week's goal? List specific actions you'll START or STOP doing next week.

Based on your progress this week, what is one micro-goal you are committed to completing next week?

When you achieve next week's goal, how will you reward yourself and celebrate your progress?

I AM WORTHY OF RECEIVING ALL OF MY GREATEST DESIRES, BIGGEST DREAMS, AND ALIGNED OPPORTUNITIES THAT ARE YET TO BE DISCOVERED.

DAY 22 Date

Morning

My top priority goal for this week is:

The three most critical actions I can take today to achieve this result:

- ❑
- ❑
- ❑

Next Steps

Evening

Something I am grateful for that helped propel me forward today:

Something I learned I can improve moving forward:

Notes & Thoughts

DAY 23 Date

Morning

My top priority goal for this week is:

The three most critical actions I can take today to achieve this result:

- ❑
- ❑
- ❑

Next Steps

Evening

Something I am grateful for that helped propel me forward today:

Something I learned I can improve moving forward:

Notes & Thoughts

DAY 24 Date

Morning

My top priority goal for this week is:

The three most critical actions I can take today to achieve this result:

- ❑
- ❑
- ❑

Next Steps

Evening

Something I am grateful for that helped propel me forward today:

Something I learned I can improve moving forward:

Notes & Thoughts

DAY 25 Date

Morning

My top priority goal for this week is:

The three most critical actions I can take today to achieve this result:

- [ ]
- [ ]
- [ ]

Next Steps

Evening

Something I am grateful for that helped propel me forward today:

Something I learned I can improve moving forward:

Notes & Thoughts

DAY 26 Date

Morning

My top priority goal for this week is:

The three most critical actions I can take today to achieve this result:

- ☐
- ☐
- ☐

Next Steps

Evening

Something I am grateful for that helped propel me forward today:

Something I learned I can improve moving forward:

Notes & Thoughts

DAY 27 Date

Morning

My top priority goal for this week is:

The three most critical actions I can take today to achieve this result:

- ❑
- ❑
- ❑

Next Steps

Evening

Something I am grateful for that helped propel me forward today:

Something I learned I can improve moving forward:

Notes & Thoughts

DAY 28 Check-In

How has setting and pursuing smaller, short-term goals each week contributed to making progress toward your long-term goal?

Over the last month, what have you learned that supports you to build momentum, stay on track, and hold yourself accountable to follow through on what's most important to you?

Does your bigger goal still hold the same significance for you? If so, why is this still important for you to pursue and achieve? If not, how has it shifted, and what about your goal might you modify in order for it to feel more aligned for you moving forward?

What is one self-care practice that, if done consistently, would support making the process of achieving your long-term goals easier? ______

______

______

Reflecting on the past month, what is the thing you are most proud of accomplishing, creating, becoming, or doing? How will you celebrate this amazing progress in a special and memorable way? ______

______

______

______

My S.M.A.R.T. goal for the upcoming month is: ______

______

______

______

I AM CAPABLE OF SETTING COURAGEOUS GOALS AND ACHIEVING THEM. I AM SURPRISING MYSELF WITH MY OWN BRILLIANCE, POWER, AND ABILITIES AS I PURSUE MY GOALS.

DAY 29 Date

Morning

My top priority goal for this week is:

The three most critical actions I can take today to achieve this result:

- ❑
- ❑
- ❑

Next Steps

Evening

Something I am grateful for that helped propel me forward today:

Something I learned I can improve moving forward:

Notes & Thoughts

DAY 30 Date

Morning

My top priority goal for this week is:

The three most critical actions I can take today to achieve this result:

- ❑
- ❑
- ❑

Next Steps

Evening

Something I am grateful for that helped propel me forward today:

Something I learned I can improve moving forward:

Notes & Thoughts

DAY 31 Date

Morning

My top priority goal for this week is:

The three most critical actions I can take today to achieve this result:

- ❑
- ❑
- ❑

Next Steps

Evening

Something I am grateful for that helped propel me forward today:

Something I learned I can improve moving forward:

Notes & Thoughts

DAY 32 Date

Morning

My top priority goal for this week is:

The three most critical actions I can take today to achieve this result:

- ❑
- ❑
- ❑

Next Steps

Evening

Something I am grateful for that helped propel me forward today:

Something I learned I can improve moving forward:

Notes & Thoughts

DAY 33 Date

Morning

My top priority goal for this week is:

The three most critical actions I can take today to achieve this result:

- [ ]
- [ ]
- [ ]

Next Steps

Evening

Something I am grateful for that helped propel me forward today:

Something I learned I can improve moving forward:

Notes & Thoughts

DAY 34 Date

Morning

My top priority goal for this week is:

The three most critical actions I can take today to achieve this result:

- ❑
- ❑
- ❑

Next Steps

Evening

Something I am grateful for that helped propel me forward today:

Something I learned I can improve moving forward:

Notes & Thoughts

DAY 35 Check-In

Did you accomplish last week's goal? YES ❑ NO ❑

On a scale of 1 to 10 (1 = least amount of effort, 10 = most amount of effort), how much effort did you commit to achieving last week's goal? ______

What did you learn about yourself in the process of pursuing last week's goal, regardless of the outcome? ______

What is one habit, thought, pattern, behavior, or practice that you've learned works well for you and feels supportive in pursuit of your goal? What's something that feels unsupportive, or as though it counteracts your progress in pursuit of your goal?

How are you committed to shifting your approach to accomplishing next week's goal? ______

What would it look like for you to show up fully (at a level 10 effort) toward next week's goal? List specific actions you'll START or STOP doing next week.

Based on your progress this week, what is one micro-goal you are committed to completing next week?

When you achieve next week's goal, how will you reward yourself and celebrate your progress?

I AM RESILIENT IN THE FACE OF THE CHALLENGES THAT TEST MY DEDICATION AND RESOLVE IN MY PURSUIT OF GREATNESS.

DAY 36 Date

Morning

My top priority goal for this week is:

The three most critical actions I can take today to achieve this result:

- ❑
- ❑
- ❑

Next Steps

Evening

Something I am grateful for that helped propel me forward today:

Something I learned I can improve moving forward:

Notes & Thoughts

DAY 37 Date

Morning

My top priority goal for this week is:

The three most critical actions I can take today to achieve this result:

- ❑
- ❑
- ❑

Next Steps

Evening

Something I am grateful for that helped propel me forward today:

Something I learned I can improve moving forward:

Notes & Thoughts

DAY 38 Date

Morning

My top priority goal for this week is:

The three most critical actions I can take today to achieve this result:

- ❑
- ❑
- ❑

Next Steps

Evening

Something I am grateful for that helped propel me forward today:

Something I learned I can improve moving forward:

Notes & Thoughts

DAY 39 Date

Morning

My top priority goal for this week is:

The three most critical actions I can take today to achieve this result:

- ☐
- ☐
- ☐

Next Steps

Evening

Something I am grateful for that helped propel me forward today:

Something I learned I can improve moving forward:

Notes & Thoughts

DAY 40 Date

Morning

My top priority goal for this week is:

The three most critical actions I can take today to achieve this result:

- ❑
- ❑
- ❑

Next Steps

Evening

Something I am grateful for that helped propel me forward today:

Something I learned I can improve moving forward:

Notes & Thoughts

DAY 41 Date

Morning

My top priority goal for this week is:

The three most critical actions I can take today to achieve this result:

- ❑
- ❑
- ❑

Next Steps

Evening

Something I am grateful for that helped propel me forward today:

Something I learned I can improve moving forward:

Notes & Thoughts

DAY 42 Check-In

Did you accomplish last week's goal? YES ❑ NO ❑

On a scale of 1 to 10 (1 = least amount of effort, 10 = most amount of effort), how much effort did you commit to achieving last week's goal? ______

What did you learn about yourself in the process of pursuing last week's goal, regardless of the outcome? ______

What is one habit, thought, pattern, behavior, or practice that you've learned works well for you and feels supportive in pursuit of your goal? What's something that feels unsupportive, or as though it counteracts your progress in pursuit of your goal?

How are you committed to shifting your approach to accomplishing next week's goal? ______

What would it look like for you to show up fully (at a level 10 effort) toward next week's goal? List specific actions you'll START or STOP doing next week.

Based on your progress this week, what is one micro-goal you are committed to completing next week?

When you achieve next week's goal, how will you reward yourself and celebrate your progress?

I AM GRATEFUL FOR THE INVITATIONS I RECEIVE FROM LIFE TO IMPROVE MYSELF AND REFINE MY APPROACH AS I MOVE CLOSER TO ACHIEVING MY GOALS, EVEN WHEN IT FEELS CHALLENGING.

DAY 43 Date

Morning

My top priority goal for this week is:

The three most critical actions I can take today to achieve this result:

- ❑
- ❑
- ❑

Next Steps

Evening

Something I am grateful for that helped propel me forward today:

Something I learned I can improve moving forward:

Notes & Thoughts

DAY 44 Date ____

Morning

My top priority goal for this week is: ____

The three most critical actions I can take today to achieve this result:

- [ ] ____
- [ ] ____
- [ ] ____

Next Steps

Evening

Something I am grateful for that helped propel me forward today:

Something I learned I can improve moving forward:

Notes & Thoughts

DAY 45 Date

Morning

My top priority goal for this week is:

The three most critical actions I can take today to achieve this result:

- ❑
- ❑
- ❑

Next Steps

Evening

Something I am grateful for that helped propel me forward today:

Something I learned I can improve moving forward:

Notes & Thoughts

DAY 46 Date

Morning

My top priority goal for this week is:

The three most critical actions I can take today to achieve this result:

- ❑
- ❑
- ❑

Next Steps

Evening

Something I am grateful for that helped propel me forward today:

Something I learned I can improve moving forward:

Notes & Thoughts

DAY 47 Date

Morning

My top priority goal for this week is:

The three most critical actions I can take today to achieve this result:

- ❑
- ❑
- ❑

Next Steps

Evening

Something I am grateful for that helped propel me forward today:

Something I learned I can improve moving forward:

Notes & Thoughts

DAY 48 Date

Morning

My top priority goal for this week is:

The three most critical actions I can take today to achieve this result:

- ❑
- ❑
- ❑

Next Steps

Evening

Something I am grateful for that helped propel me forward today:

Something I learned I can improve moving forward:

Notes & Thoughts

DAY 49 Check-In

Did you accomplish last week's goal? YES ❑ NO ❑

On a scale of 1 to 10 (1 = least amount of effort, 10 = most amount of effort), how much effort did you commit to achieving last week's goal? __________

What did you learn about yourself in the process of pursuing last week's goal, regardless of the outcome? __________

What is one habit, thought, pattern, behavior, or practice that you've learned works well for you and feels supportive in pursuit of your goal? What's something that feels unsupportive, or as though it counteracts your progress in pursuit of your goal?

How are you committed to shifting your approach to accomplishing next week's goal? __________

What would it look like for you to show up fully (at a level 10 effort) toward next week's goal? List specific actions you'll START or STOP doing next week.

Based on your progress this week, what is one micro-goal you are committed to completing next week?

When you achieve next week's goal, how will you reward yourself and celebrate your progress?

I AM OPEN AND AVAILABLE TO RECEIVING CREATIVE SOLUTIONS. I SURRENDER TO ALL OUTCOMES AND SITUATIONS THAT ARE OUTSIDE OF MY CONTROL AND FREELY ALLOW MYSELF TO BE GUIDED FORWARD.

DAY 50 Date

Morning

My top priority goal for this week is:

The three most critical actions I can take today to achieve this result:

- ❑
- ❑
- ❑

Next Steps

Evening

Something I am grateful for that helped propel me forward today:

Something I learned I can improve moving forward:

Notes & Thoughts

DAY 51 Date

Morning

My top priority goal for this week is:

The three most critical actions I can take today to achieve this result:

- ❑
- ❑
- ❑

Next Steps

Evening

Something I am grateful for that helped propel me forward today:

Something I learned I can improve moving forward:

Notes & Thoughts

DAY 52 Date

Morning

My top priority goal for this week is:

The three most critical actions I can take today to achieve this result:

- ❑
- ❑
- ❑

Next Steps

Evening

Something I am grateful for that helped propel me forward today:

Something I learned I can improve moving forward:

Notes & Thoughts

DAY 53 Date

Morning

My top priority goal for this week is:

The three most critical actions I can take today to achieve this result:

- ☐
- ☐
- ☐

Next Steps

Evening

Something I am grateful for that helped propel me forward today:

Something I learned I can improve moving forward:

Notes & Thoughts

DAY 54 Date

Morning

My top priority goal for this week is:

The three most critical actions I can take today to achieve this result:

- ❑
- ❑
- ❑

Next Steps

Evening

Something I am grateful for that helped propel me forward today:

Something I learned I can improve moving forward:

Notes & Thoughts

DAY 55 Date

Morning

My top priority goal for this week is:

The three most critical actions I can take today to achieve this result:

- ❑
- ❑
- ❑

Next Steps

Evening

Something I am grateful for that helped propel me forward today:

Something I learned I can improve moving forward:

Notes & Thoughts

DAY 56 Check-In

Did you accomplish last week's goal? YES ❑ NO ❑

On a scale of 1 to 10 (1 = least amount of effort, 10 = most amount of effort), how much effort did you commit to achieving last week's goal? ______

What did you learn about yourself in the process of pursuing last week's goal, regardless of the outcome? ______

What is one habit, thought, pattern, behavior, or practice that you've learned works well for you and feels supportive in pursuit of your goal? What's something that feels unsupportive, or as though it counteracts your progress in pursuit of your goal?

How are you committed to shifting your approach to accomplishing next week's goal? ______

What would it look like for you to show up fully (at a level 10 effort) toward next week's goal? List specific actions you'll START or STOP doing next week.

Based on your progress this week, what is one micro-goal you are committed to completing next week?

When you achieve next week's goal, how will you reward yourself and celebrate your progress?

I AM NATURALLY EXPANDING POSSIBILITY, OPPORTUNITY, AND EASE IN PURSUIT OF MY GOALS. I ALLOW MY JOURNEY TO BE FILLED WITH JOY, BEAUTY, AND WONDER.

DAY 57 Date

Morning

My top priority goal for this week is:

The three most critical actions I can take today to achieve this result:

- ❑
- ❑
- ❑

Next Steps

Evening

Something I am grateful for that helped propel me forward today:

Something I learned I can improve moving forward:

Notes & Thoughts

DAY 58 Date

Morning

My top priority goal for this week is:

The three most critical actions I can take today to achieve this result:

- ❑
- ❑
- ❑

Next Steps

Evening

Something I am grateful for that helped propel me forward today:

Something I learned I can improve moving forward:

Notes & Thoughts

DAY 59 Date

Morning

My top priority goal for this week is:

The three most critical actions I can take today to achieve this result:

- [ ]
- [ ]
- [ ]

Next Steps

Evening

Something I am grateful for that helped propel me forward today:

Something I learned I can improve moving forward:

Notes & Thoughts

DAY 60 Date

Morning

My top priority goal for this week is:

The three most critical actions I can take today to achieve this result:

- ❑
- ❑
- ❑

Next Steps

Evening

Something I am grateful for that helped propel me forward today:

Something I learned I can improve moving forward:

Notes & Thoughts

DAY 61 Date

Morning

My top priority goal for this week is:

The three most critical actions I can take today to achieve this result:

- ☐
- ☐
- ☐

Next Steps

Evening

Something I am grateful for that helped propel me forward today:

Something I learned I can improve moving forward:

Notes & Thoughts

DAY 62 Date

Morning

My top priority goal for this week is:

The three most critical actions I can take today to achieve this result:

- ☐
- ☐
- ☐

Next Steps

Evening

Something I am grateful for that helped propel me forward today:

Something I learned I can improve moving forward:

Notes & Thoughts

DAY 63 Check-In

Did you accomplish last week's goal? YES ❑ NO ❑

On a scale of 1 to 10 (1 = least amount of effort, 10 = most amount of effort), how much effort did you commit to achieving last week's goal?

What did you learn about yourself in the process of pursuing last week's goal, regardless of the outcome?

What is one habit, thought, pattern, behavior, or practice that you've learned works well for you and feels supportive in pursuit of your goal? What's something that feels unsupportive, or as though it counteracts your progress in pursuit of your goal?

How are you committed to shifting your approach to accomplishing next week's goal?

What would it look like for you to show up fully (at a level 10 effort) toward next week's goal? List specific actions you'll START or STOP doing next week.

Based on your progress this week, what is one micro-goal you are committed to completing next week?

When you achieve next week's goal, how will you reward yourself and celebrate your progress?

I GRACEFULLY EMBRACE AND AM OPEN TO THE LESSONS THAT ARE SUPPORTING ME TO GROW, EVOLVE, AND LEVEL UP INTO THE VERSION OF MYSELF THAT I AM BECOMING.

DAY 64 Date

Morning

My top priority goal for this week is:

The three most critical actions I can take today to achieve this result:

- [ ]
- [ ]
- [ ]

Next Steps

Evening

Something I am grateful for that helped propel me forward today:

Something I learned I can improve moving forward:

Notes & Thoughts

DAY 65 Date

Morning

My top priority goal for this week is:

The three most critical actions I can take today to achieve this result:

- [ ]
- [ ]
- [ ]

Next Steps

Evening

Something I am grateful for that helped propel me forward today:

Something I learned I can improve moving forward:

Notes & Thoughts

DAY 66 Date

Morning

My top priority goal for this week is:

The three most critical actions I can take today to achieve this result:

- ❑
- ❑
- ❑

Next Steps

Evening

Something I am grateful for that helped propel me forward today:

Something I learned I can improve moving forward:

Notes & Thoughts

DAY 67 Date

Morning

My top priority goal for this week is:

The three most critical actions I can take today to achieve this result:

- [ ]
- [ ]
- [ ]

Next Steps

Evening

Something I am grateful for that helped propel me forward today:

Something I learned I can improve moving forward:

Notes & Thoughts

DAY 68 Date

Morning

My top priority goal for this week is:

The three most critical actions I can take today to achieve this result:

- [ ]
- [ ]
- [ ]

Next Steps

Evening

Something I am grateful for that helped propel me forward today:

Something I learned I can improve moving forward:

Notes & Thoughts

DAY 69 Date

Morning

My top priority goal for this week is:

The three most critical actions I can take today to achieve this result:

- ❑
- ❑
- ❑

Next Steps

Evening

Something I am grateful for that helped propel me forward today:

Something I learned I can improve moving forward:

Notes & Thoughts

DAY 70 Check-In

Did you accomplish last week's goal? YES ❑ NO ❑

On a scale of 1 to 10 (1 = least amount of effort, 10 = most amount of effort), how much effort did you commit to achieving last week's goal? __________

What did you learn about yourself in the process of pursuing last week's goal, regardless of the outcome? __________

What is one habit, thought, pattern, behavior, or practice that you've learned works well for you and feels supportive in pursuit of your goal? What's something that feels unsupportive, or as though it counteracts your progress in pursuit of your goal?

How are you committed to shifting your approach to accomplishing next week's goal? __________

What would it look like for you to show up fully (at a level 10 effort) toward next week's goal? List specific actions you'll START or STOP doing next week.

Based on your progress this week, what is one micro-goal you are committed to completing next week?

When you achieve next week's goal, how will you reward yourself and celebrate your progress?

I RELEASE THE DESIRE TO SEEK THE APPROVAL OR PERMISSION OF OTHERS TO MAKE ALIGNED CHOICES AND TAKE INTENTIONAL ACTION IN MY LIFE.

DAY 71 Date

Morning

My top priority goal for this week is:

The three most critical actions I can take today to achieve this result:

- ❑
- ❑
- ❑

Next Steps

Evening

Something I am grateful for that helped propel me forward today:

Something I learned I can improve moving forward:

Notes & Thoughts

DAY 72 Date

Morning

My top priority goal for this week is:

The three most critical actions I can take today to achieve this result:

- ❑
- ❑
- ❑

Next Steps

Evening

Something I am grateful for that helped propel me forward today:

Something I learned I can improve moving forward:

Notes & Thoughts

DAY 73 Date

Morning

My top priority goal for this week is:

The three most critical actions I can take today to achieve this result:

- ❑
- ❑
- ❑

Next Steps

Evening

Something I am grateful for that helped propel me forward today:

Something I learned I can improve moving forward:

Notes & Thoughts

DAY 74 Date

Morning

My top priority goal for this week is:

The three most critical actions I can take today to achieve this result:

- ❑
- ❑
- ❑

Next Steps

Evening

Something I am grateful for that helped propel me forward today:

Something I learned I can improve moving forward:

Notes & Thoughts

DAY 75 Date

Morning

My top priority goal for this week is:

The three most critical actions I can take today to achieve this result:

- ❑
- ❑
- ❑

Next Steps

Evening

Something I am grateful for that helped propel me forward today:

Something I learned I can improve moving forward:

Notes & Thoughts

DAY 76 Date

Morning

My top priority goal for this week is:

The three most critical actions I can take today to achieve this result:

- ❑
- ❑
- ❑

Next Steps

Evening

Something I am grateful for that helped propel me forward today:

Something I learned I can improve moving forward:

Notes & Thoughts

DAY 77 Check-In

Did you accomplish last week's goal? YES ❑ NO ❑

On a scale of 1 to 10 (1 = least amount of effort, 10 = most amount of effort), how much effort did you commit to achieving last week's goal? ______

What did you learn about yourself in the process of pursuing last week's goal, regardless of the outcome? ______

What is one habit, thought, pattern, behavior, or practice that you've learned works well for you and feels supportive in pursuit of your goal? What's something that feels unsupportive, or as though it counteracts your progress in pursuit of your goal?

How are you committed to shifting your approach to accomplishing next week's goal? ______

What would it look like for you to show up fully (at a level 10 effort) toward next week's goal? List specific actions you'll START or STOP doing next week.

Based on your progress this week, what is one micro-goal you are committed to completing next week?

When you achieve next week's goal, how will you reward yourself and celebrate your progress?

I ACTIVELY CHOOSE TO RELEASE FEAR, RESISTANCE, AND WORRY IN ORDER TO CULTIVATE ABUNDANCE, LOVE, AND JOY.

DAY 78 Date

Morning

My top priority goal for this week is:

The three most critical actions I can take today to achieve this result:

- ❑
- ❑
- ❑

Next Steps

Evening

Something I am grateful for that helped propel me forward today:

Something I learned I can improve moving forward:

Notes & Thoughts

DAY 79 Date

Morning

My top priority goal for this week is:

The three most critical actions I can take today to achieve this result:

- ☐
- ☐
- ☐

Next Steps

Evening

Something I am grateful for that helped propel me forward today:

Something I learned I can improve moving forward:

Notes & Thoughts

DAY 80 Date

Morning

My top priority goal for this week is:

The three most critical actions I can take today to achieve this result:

- ❑
- ❑
- ❑

Next Steps

Evening

Something I am grateful for that helped propel me forward today:

Something I learned I can improve moving forward:

Notes & Thoughts

DAY 81 Date

Morning

My top priority goal for this week is:

The three most critical actions I can take today to achieve this result:

- ☐
- ☐
- ☐

Next Steps

Evening

Something I am grateful for that helped propel me forward today:

Something I learned I can improve moving forward:

Notes & Thoughts

DAY 82 Date

Morning

My top priority goal for this week is:

The three most critical actions I can take today to achieve this result:

- ☐
- ☐
- ☐

Next Steps

Evening

Something I am grateful for that helped propel me forward today:

Something I learned I can improve moving forward:

Notes & Thoughts

DAY 83 Date

Morning

My top priority goal for this week is:

The three most critical actions I can take today to achieve this result:

- [ ]
- [ ]
- [ ]

Next Steps

Evening

Something I am grateful for that helped propel me forward today:

Something I learned I can improve moving forward:

Notes & Thoughts

DAY 84 Check-In

Did you accomplish last week's goal? YES ❑ NO ❑

On a scale of 1 to 10 (1 = least amount of effort, 10 = most amount of effort), how much effort did you commit to achieving last week's goal? ______

What did you learn about yourself in the process of pursuing last week's goal, regardless of the outcome? ______

What is one habit, thought, pattern, behavior, or practice that you've learned works well for you and feels supportive in pursuit of your goal? What's something that feels unsupportive, or as though it counteracts your progress in pursuit of your goal?

How are you committed to shifting your approach to accomplishing next week's goal? ______

What would it look like for you to show up fully (at a level 10 effort) toward next week's goal? List specific actions you'll START or STOP doing next week.

Based on your progress this week, what is one micro-goal you are committed to completing next week?

When you achieve next week's goal, how will you reward yourself and celebrate your progress?

I AM A MAGNET FOR MY DESIRES, DREAMS, AND GOALS. I AM WORTHY, DESERVING, AND ENOUGH JUST AS I AM. MY PATH UNFOLDS IN PERFECT TIMING.

DAY 85 Date

Morning

My top priority goal for this week is:

The three most critical actions I can take today to achieve this result:

- ☐
- ☐
- ☐

Next Steps

Evening

Something I am grateful for that helped propel me forward today:

Something I learned I can improve moving forward:

Notes & Thoughts

DAY 86 Date

Morning

My top priority goal for this week is:

The three most critical actions I can take today to achieve this result:

- ❑
- ❑
- ❑

Next Steps

Evening

Something I am grateful for that helped propel me forward today:

Something I learned I can improve moving forward:

Notes & Thoughts

DAY 87 Date

Morning

My top priority goal for this week is:

The three most critical actions I can take today to achieve this result:

- ❑
- ❑
- ❑

Next Steps

Evening

Something I am grateful for that helped propel me forward today:

Something I learned I can improve moving forward:

Notes & Thoughts

DAY 88 Date

Morning

My top priority goal for this week is:

The three most critical actions I can take today to achieve this result:

- ☐
- ☐
- ☐

Next Steps

Evening

Something I am grateful for that helped propel me forward today:

Something I learned I can improve moving forward:

Notes & Thoughts

DAY 89 Date

Morning

My top priority goal for this week is:

The three most critical actions I can take today to achieve this result:

- ❑
- ❑
- ❑

Next Steps

Evening

Something I am grateful for that helped propel me forward today:

Something I learned I can improve moving forward:

Notes & Thoughts

DAY 90 Check-In

Did you accomplish the S.M.A.R.T. goal(s) you set out to over the past 90 days? YES ❑ NO ❑

What is the most important lesson you'd like to carry forward with you after these 90 days of committing to your growth?

What are you most grateful for that's occurred over the last 90 days?

What new positive habits or behaviors are you most proud of yourself for adopting over the last 90 days? What are you most proud of yourself for releasing, letting go of, or stopping during this time?

Who have you become in the process of setting and pursuing your goal? Who have you un-become in this process?

Congratulations and Final Thoughts

Congratulations! You have successfully completed the task of tracking your goals over the past 90 days. I hope you're feeling proud of yourself, accomplished, and inspired by the progress you've made!

Whether you achieved exactly what you set out to on Day 1, or your goals pivoted throughout the course of the past three months, know that you have made tremendous change in your life and, most importantly, learned so much about yourself in the process.

Take a moment to flip back through the pages in your journal to reflect on the journey and see if anything stands out to you as memorable—perhaps a moment that was a turning point for you, a moment of questioning or doubt, or a moment of a significant decision. Notice how it feels to process, reflect, and remember who you were 90 days ago and who you are in this moment.

I hope that as you journey forward, you'll recall the important lessons you've discovered in this journal and keep it to refer back to over time as a token of your meaningful dedication to what matters most to you.

I recommend revisiting this journal whenever you're feeling discouraged, uninspired, or doubtful. It's also useful as a reference for how to set your next S.M.A.R.T. goals for the next 90 days, as your values or desires may have shifted.

It has been an honor to guide you through the process of setting, pursuing, and achieving S.M.A.R.T. goals!

I am devoted to
pursuing and achieving what
is the highest good for
all concerned,
including myself.

Resources

Websites

AuthenticHappiness.org
The University of Pennsylvania's hub for exploring positive psychology through helpful resources, trainings, books, and questionnaires to support living a more fulfilling life.

BreneBrown.com
Brené Brown is a researcher, author of five number-one *New York Times* bestsellers, podcast host, and storyteller. Visit her website to explore her free resources, take the Wholehearted Inventory, tune in to her podcasts, and purchase her books.

EmilyCassel.com/free
A curated library of free tools, resources, and training to help you take a business idea to launch, grow or scale an existing business, and activate your soul's mission.

Journals

***Habits: A 12-Week Journal to Change Your Habits, Track Your Progress, and Achieve Your Goals* by Dr. Hayden Finch**
The Habits journal, written by psychologist and behavior change expert Dr. Hayden Finch, provides a clear, manageable path to setting achievable goals over the course of 12 weeks.

***The 5-Minute Motivational Journal: Daily Prompts to Achieve Your Goals and Live Intentionally* by Dr. Christian Rizea PsyD**
This journal is filled with prompts, exercises, and quotes to help you assess your priorities and make positive changes in yourself and your surroundings—in just 5 minutes each day.

The Self-Discovery Journal: 52 Weeks of Reflection, Inspiration, and Growth **by Dr. Yana Lechtman PsyD**
In this journal, a year of weekly quotes and writing prompts encourage you to look honestly at your relationship with yourself and the world around you. As you come to understand your own nature and motivations, you'll learn what to let go of—and what you need to grow and flourish.

5-Minute Manifesting Journal: Focus Your Mind, Raise Your Vibration, and Turn Your Dreams Into Reality **by Scott Moore**
This journal helps you develop your manifestation practice through short, daily prompts that encourage you to express what you want out of today, what you're thankful for, and what you can do to get more out of tomorrow.

Dream Big: A Five-Minute Goal Journal **by Karl W. Gruber**
This guided goal journal harnesses the power of visualization to help manifest your dreams, and shows you that even five minutes of reflection can work wonders in your life.

Acknowledgments

I am deeply grateful to my teachers, clients, soul family, and team members of the past, present, and future whose hands and hearts have brought life to this book. It has been a privilege to serve you, cocreate with you, learn from you, support, and be supported by you.

The utmost appreciation to my grandfather Kevin Gaut, who was my first and forever teacher in so many ways. Thank you for gifting me with your presence, your care, and your relentless desire to improve and to serve during this lifetime. How fortunate I am to have shared 20 years under your wing.

To all the wisdom-keepers, way-showers, and teachers in all their forms, both animate and inanimate, thank you for sharing your guidance.

Deep thanks to all the devoted dreamers, changemakers, and visionaries called to blaze new trails for future generations; you inspire me to continue to stay on my path and in my truest work, despite the challenges and growth edges of the entrepreneurial way.

About the Author

Emily Cassel is a Soulful Business + Leadership Coach, podcast host, and retreat leader based in Charleston, South Carolina.

Emily activates and alchemizes women entrepreneurs from across the globe and their businesses through her signature coaching experiences, including The Soulful Business Academy and The Soulful Leadership Mastermind.

She is the author of the *52-Week Motivational Journal: Prompts and Exercises to Inspire, Motivate, and Help You Achieve Your Goals* (Rockridge Press, 2021). Learn more about Emily's work and receive free tools, resources, and training at EmilyCassel.com.